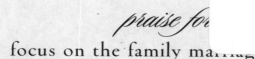

This marriage study series is pure Focus on the Family—
reliable, biblically sound and dedicated to reestablishing family values
in today's society. This series will no doubt help a multitude of couples
strengthen their relationship, not only with each other,
but also with God, the *creator* of marriage itself.

Bruce Wilkinson

Author, The BreakThrough Series: *The Prayer of Jabez,*
Secrets of the Vine and *A Life God Rewards*

In this era of such need, Dr. Dobson's team has produced solid,
helpful materials about Christian marriage. Even if they have been
through marriage studies before, every couple—married or engaged—
will benefit from this foundational study of life together. Thanks to
Focus on the Family for helping set us straight in this top priority.

Charles W. Colson

Chairman, Prison Fellowship Ministries

In my 31 years as a pastor, I've officiated at hundreds of weddings.
Unfortunately, many of those unions failed. I only wish the *Focus on the*
Family Marriage Series had been available to me during those years.
What a marvelous tool you as pastors and Christian leaders have
at your disposal. I encourage you to use it to assist those you
serve in building successful, healthy marriages.

H. B. London, Jr.

Vice President, Ministry Outreach/Pastoral Ministries
Focus on the Family

Looking for a prescription for a better marriage?
You'll enjoy this timely and practical series!

Dr. Kevin Leman

Author, *Sheet Music: Uncovering the Secrets of
Sexual Intimacy in Marriage*

The *Focus on the Family Marriage Series* is successful because it shifts
the focus from how to fix or strengthen a marriage to *who* can do it.
Through this study you will learn that a blessed marriage will be the
happy by-product of a closer relationship with the *creator* of marriage.

Lisa Whelchel

Author, *Creative Correction* and
The Facts of Life and Other Lessons My Father Taught Me

In a day and age where the covenant of marriage is so quickly tossed
aside in the name of incompatibility and irreconcilable differences, a
marriage Bible study that is both inspirational and practical is desperately
needed. The *Focus on the Family Marriage Series* is what couples are seeking.
I give my highest recommendation to this Bible study series that has the
potential to dramatically impact and improve marriages today. Marriage
is not so much about finding the right partner as it is about being the
right partner. These studies give wonderful biblical teachings for
helping those who want to learn the beautiful art of being and
becoming all that God intends in their marriage.

Lysa TerKeurst

President, Proverbs 31 Ministries
Author, *Capture His Heart* and *Capture Her Heart*

focus on the family® marriage series

the blended marriage

Gospel Light

Gospel Light is a Christian publisher dedicated to serving the local church. We believe God's vision for Gospel Light is to provide church leaders with biblical, user-friendly materials that will help them evangelize, disciple and minister to children, youth and families.

It is our prayer that this Gospel Light resource will help you discover biblical truth for your own life and help you minister to others. May God richly bless you.

For a free catalog of resources from Gospel Light, please call your Christian supplier or contact us at 1-800-4-GOSPEL *or* www.gospellight.com

PUBLISHING STAFF
William T. Greig, Chairman · **Dr. Elmer L. Towns,** Senior Consulting Publisher · **Natalie Clark,** Product Line Manager · **Pam Weston,** Managing Editor · **Hilary Young,** Editorial Assistant · **Jessie Minassian,** Editorial Assistant · **Bayard Taylor, M.Div.,** Senior Editor, Biblical and Theological Issues · **Rosanne Moreland,** Cover and Internal Designer · **Debbie Alsdorf,** Contributing Writer

table of contents

Foreword by Gary T. Smalley 6

Introduction 8

Session One: Living the Unexpected—Romans 8:35,37 11
> Living through the unexpected twists and turns of remarriage
> requires putting Christ solidly at the center of the relationship.

Session Two: Living with New Challenges—
2 Corinthians 12:9-10 25
> In the midst of misunderstandings, rearranged family
> dynamics and the tug-of-war that goes on in blending
> families, the hope of Christ's presence with us is great
> news.

Session Three: Living with New Relationships—1 John 4:16 40
> In remarriage we say "I do" to more than just our spouse;
> there are children, exes, in-laws and ex-in-laws to deal with.
> Christ is our example as we learn to show His love in
> difficult relationships.

Session Four: Living with New Hope—Romans 15:13 53
> Statistics clearly show that remarriages struggle to
> survive. However, in Christ we can be more than another
> statistic—we have hope because He dwells within us!

Leader's Discussion Guide 67

foreword

The most urgent mission field on Earth is not across the sea or even across the street—it's right where you live: in your home and family. Jesus' last instruction was to "make disciples of all nations" (Matthew 28:19). At the thought of this command, our eyes look across the world for our work field. That's not bad; it's just not *all*. God intended the home to be the first place of Christian discipleship and growth (see Deuteronomy 6:4-8). Our family members must be the *first* ones we reach out to in word and example with the gospel of the Lord Jesus Christ, and the fundamental way in which this occurs is through the marriage relationship.

Divorce, blended families, the breakdown of communication and the complexities of daily life are taking a devastating toll on the God-ordained institutions of marriage and family. We do not need to look hard or search far for evidence that even Christian marriages and families are also in a desperate state. In response to the need to build strong Christ-centered marriages and families, this series was developed.

Focus on the Family is well known and respected worldwide for its steadfast dedication to preserving the sanctity of marriage and family life. I can think of no better partnership than the one formed by Focus on the Family and Gospel Light to produce the *Focus on the Family Marriage Series*. This series is well written, biblically sound and right on target for guiding couples to explore the foundation God has laid for marriage and to see Him as the role model for the perfect spouse. Through these studies, seeds will be planted that will germinate in your heart and mind for many years to come.

In our practical, bottom-line culture, we often want to jump over the *why* and get straight to the *what*. We think that by *doing* the six steps or *learning* the five ways, we will reach the goal. But deep-rooted growth is slower and more purposeful and begins with a well-grounded understanding of God's divine design. Knowing why marriage exists is crucial to making the how-tos more effective. Marriage is a gift from God, a unique and distinct covenant relationship through which His glory and goodness can resonate, and it is only through knowing the architect and His plan that we will build our marriage on the surest foundation.

God created marriage; He has a specific purpose for it, and He is committed to filling with fresh life and renewed strength each union yielded to Him. God wants to gather the hearts of every couple together, unite them in love and walk them to the finish line—all in His great grace and goodness.

May God, in His grace, lead you into His truth, strengthening your lives and your marriage.

Gary T. Smalley
Founder and Chairman of the Board
Smalley Relationship Center

introduction

At the beginning of creation God "made them male and female." "For this reason a man will leave his father and mother and be united to his wife, and the two will become one flesh." So they are no longer two, but one.

Mark 10:6-8

The Blended Marriage can be used in a variety of situations, including small-group Bible studies, Sunday School classes or counseling or mentoring situations. An individual couple can also use this book as an at-home marriage-building study.

Each of the four sessions contains four main components.

Session Overview

Tilling the Ground

This is an introduction to the topic being discussed—commentary and questions to direct your thoughts toward the main idea of the session.

Planting the Seed

This is the Bible study portion in which you will read Scripture and answer questions to help discover lasting truths from God's Word.

Watering the Hope

This is a time for discussion and prayer. Whether you are using the study at home as a couple, in a small group or in a classroom setting, talking about the lesson with your spouse is a great way to solidify the truth and plant it deeply in your hearts.

As a point of action, this portion of the session offers suggestions on putting the truth of the Word into action in your marriage relationship.

Suggestions for Individual Couple Study

There are at least three options for using this study as a couple.

- It may be used as a devotional study that each spouse would study individually through the week; then on a specified day, come together and discuss what you have learned and how to apply it to your marriage.
- You might choose to study one session together in an evening and then work on the application activities during the rest of the week.
- Because of the short length of this study, it is a great resource for a weekend retreat. Take a trip away for the weekend, and study each session together, interspersed with your favorite leisure activities.

Suggestions for Group Study

There are many ways that this study can be used in a group situation. The most common way is in a small-group Bible study format. However, it can also be used in an adult Sunday School class. However you choose to use it, there are some general guidelines to follow for group study.

- Keep the group small—five to six couples is probably the maximum.
- Ask couples to commit to regular attendance for the four weeks of the study. Regular attendance is a key to building relationships and trust in a group.
- Encourage participants *not* to share anything of a personal or potentially embarrassing nature without first asking the spouse's permission.

- Whatever is discussed in the group meetings is to be held in strictest confidence among group members only.

There are additional leader helps in the back of this book and in *The Focus on the Family Marriage Ministry Guide*.

Suggestions for Mentoring or Counseling Relationships

This study also lends itself for use in relationships where one couple mentors or counsels another couple.

- A mentoring relationship, where a couple that has been married for several years is assigned to meet on a regular basis with a younger couple, could be arranged through a system set up by a church or ministry.
- A less formal way to start a mentoring relationship is for a younger couple to take the initiative and approach a couple that exemplifies a mature, godly marriage and ask them to meet with them on a regular basis. Or the reverse might be a mature couple that approaches a younger couple to begin a mentoring relationship.
- When asked to mentor, some might shy away and think that they could never do that, knowing that their own marriage is less than perfect. But just as we are to disciple new believers, we must learn to disciple married couples to strengthen marriages in this difficult world. The Lord has promised to be "with you always" (Matthew 28:20).
- Before you begin to mentor a couple, first complete the study yourselves. This will serve to strengthen your own marriage and prepare you for leading another couple.
- Be prepared to learn as much or more than the couple(s) you will mentor.

There are additional helps for mentoring relationships in *The Focus on the Family Marriage Ministry Guide*.

living the
unexpected

Who shall separate us from the love of Christ? Shall trouble or hardship or persecution or famine or nakedness or danger or sword? No, in all these things we are more than conquerors through him who loved us.
Romans 8:35,37

Death of the *dream* is the common thread weaving through a blended marriage. Most people don't grow up with a wish to be married more than once. The typical dream is to meet the right person, fall in love, build a life together and live happily ever after. But for many the dream of happily ever after was cut short by death or divorce. Thus began the journey of starting over.

A blended marriage is foundationally different from a first marriage because it is the coming together of two people who have suffered loss and hurt in a previous relationship. We walk down the aisle with baggage that no one can see—emotional wounds and hurts from the past that threaten to prevent us from truly experiencing love again. Walls of protection that we previously built to withstand the pain of loss can now keep us self-focused and unable to fully yield ourselves to another person. While seeking another chance at love, we must realize that it is possible for this new relationship to be lived in the spirit of restoration and acceptance of what is now our new reality. The only way to survive the unexpected twists and turns of remarriage is to put Christ solidly at the center of the relationship.

tilling the ground

Our dreams shape our expectations. In every marriage relationship there are blessings as well as challenges and surprises. Examining our expectations helps us identify unrealistic thinking that might affect our relationships. Let's face it, living in the *blender* is sometimes (or some may say "often") a challenging mix of his, hers and ours, as well as in-laws and ex-laws (or is it "out-laws"?)!

1. What were your expectations as you started over in this new marriage?

   What did this new relationship and new family look like in your dream?

2. What has been the biggest surprise or concern as reality has hit your relationship?

3. In light of the challenges you have experienced so far, what has proven to be the greatest blessing in this marriage?

4. What outside forces are intruding into your home and challenging your relationship with your spouse?

Life is full of the unexpected. There are many things that we cannot control. This is especially true in a blended marriage. Often there are many circumstances involved: new family ties being formed, old family ties struggling for survival and misunderstandings along the way. Still, through all of these things, we can learn to rely on the love of Christ—a love that is deep, rich, unconditional and very real. It is His love that will enable us to go the distance while living in the unexpected and uncharted territory of a blended marriage.

planting the seed

Expectations run high in every marriage relationship. Often our expectations don't match what soon becomes our reality. Because of past circumstances and relationships, we will undoubtedly be challenged by difficult situations that we may have never anticipated. Though there are many new blessings, still the road is sometimes rocky and the path unbelievably hard. In such circumstances we are often tempted to think that even God has left us.

Not Forsaken

The apostle Paul reminds us in the book of Romans that nothing shall separate us from the love of Christ. We all go through challenges in life, but none of them can separate us from Him who loves us. And because of this promise we can also be victors rather than victims of challenges and circumstances.

5. What did Jesus Christ tell us to expect in John 16:33? And what is the promise of this verse?

The word translated "trouble" here is the Greek word *thlipsis* which can also be translated in the following ways: distress, hardships, suffering, persecution, afflictions, trials, anguish, hard pressed, severe trial, tribulations.[1]

6. What are the problems commonly experienced in a blended marriage?

The words Jesus spoke to His disciples are still pertinent to us today. If we back up to the beginning of John 16, we can see that He is warning them of hard times to come, but He clearly promises them that He will not leave them hanging out on a limb to figure things out on their own. In verses 5 through 15 He told them of the work of the Holy Spirit in their lives.

7. What does Jesus say about the work of the Holy Spirit in John 16:5-15?

How does this relate to handling difficult circumstances?

The Holy Spirit comes to lead us and guide us into all truth. Truth sets us free and enables us to take heart and to be of good cheer despite the unexpected dramas of life that occur in a blended marriage.

8. What happens inside you when your life circumstances are hard?

How can these feelings affect your marriage?

In our culture life has become "all about me" and my personal pursuit of happiness. This selfish attitude has even shaped the way we as Christians view life. However, this is not the way our life is to be viewed according to Scripture. Instead of viewing our life as being for our own pleasure, we are to live to please God. But often, in a blended marriage, because of past hurts, two people come together grasping at happiness that has seemed to elude them. The results can be devastating if the focus is not readjusted and aligned to the truth in God's Word for us as individuals who belong to Him.

9. What did the apostle Paul say about his hardships in 2 Corinthians 1:8-10?

10. According to 2 Corinthians 1:9-10, Paul was certainly feeling despair. However, even in the midst of hardship, he chose to put his hope in God's deliverance. How can this same choice affect those in a blended marriage?

There is a positive side to challenge. Scripture is clear that challenges are part of life and that they actually benefit us since they cause us to depend on God's strength in our daily world. It really is all about a focus change. Rather than focusing on the difficulties and falling into discouragement and despair, we can learn to focus on God's purpose: to change us through our difficult circumstances to be more like Christ. One view produces a feeling of being trapped; the other an assurance of empowerment to rise above and grow through the hard times.

Dealing with the Unexpected

When dealing with the unexpected, we need to keep in mind three things:

1. We must be *honest* with God, telling Him how situations hurt, how hard they are to handle, how we cannot do the right thing in our own strength, etc.
2. We must find our *hope* in His faithfulness, choosing to stand in the promises of God's Word, telling ourselves the truth and letting truth bring hope to our heart.
3. We must *humble* our heart and will to His plan for our life; humility is the pathway to being truly free. It's time to believe that God is who He says He is and that He can be trusted with everything.

Be Honest

Oftentimes we hide our true feelings, stuffing those things that we are ashamed of down deep in our hearts. This course of action will keep us stuck in despair when the unexpected strikes. Instead we are to come before God, telling Him all of our hurts, cares and longings.

11. What does 1 Peter 5:7 say we can do about our anxiety?

12. Philippians 4:4-6 gives clear instruction on what we are to do when faced with a problem. What are we commanded to do in every situation?

13. How would following these directions help a couple meet the challenges that are specific to a blended marriage?

Describe a time when you actually turned a difficult situation over to the Lord and received His help and guidance.

It's important to remember that our challenges in thought and circumstance are not unique and unconquerable. Others in similar (or perhaps even worse) situations are learning to be honest and prayerful in their blended marriage. As we learn to be honest with ourselves, our mates and the Lord, we will also learn how to turn anxiety and concern into prayer and praise. When we trust in the Lord, we will be given the peace that produces new hope.

14. In 1 Peter 5:7 we are told that we can cast all of our cares upon the Lord. How can we do that with confidence?

15. What is promised in 1 Peter 5:10?

    Have you personally experienced restoration after a difficult time? Explain what happened.

16. According to James 1:2-4, what is the purpose of trials?

    How can this passage provide hope during the challenges of a blended marriage?

"After [we] have suffered a little while" (1 Peter 5:10) is an interesting concept, isn't it? We don't want to suffer. But it is a necessary part of the life process, bringing us to restoration and actually making us complete. Suffering produces men and women of strength. It also produces people of perseverance who are able to keep their commitment and finish the course set before them.

17. What does Philippians 4:6-7 promise will happen when we take our problems and apply the "prayer, petition and thanksgiving" principle?

Having a peace that transcends understanding is an amazing promise. It means that although we don't understand the whys or hows of our current situation, we still have peace because our hope is in Christ, who is always trustworthy.

Be Humble

Jesus came to do the will of the Father. He was about His Father's business. He claimed that His life was not His own. It is through humility that we are able to lay down our own desires and dreams for the will of the One who created us for His glory.

18. How is laying down our cares and giving them to the Lord an act of humility?

19. What is the hardest thing about your marriage for you to lay down for fear that God will not work it out the way you would like it to be worked out?

20. What does 1 Peter 5:5-6 tell us to do that would help when dealing with the unexpected issues that come up in our blended marriage relationship?

21. How does pride get in the way of dealing with issues fairly?

22. How does personal pride get in the way of healing past personal hurts, emptying old emotional baggage or dealing with each other's children or relatives?

As you work through the challenges of blending your marriage, you can trust in the Lord to meet your needs and help you come through the tough times stronger. Remember to be honest, be hopeful and be humble.

The challenges in a blended marriage will take us where the rubber meets the road in our daily lives. It is easy to walk by faith when everything is fine. It's not so easy to walk by faith when God calls us to live in ways that go against the grain of our flesh or our pride. Our flesh and pride long for happiness at all costs. In any marriage this could cause a lot of problems, but in a blended marriage there may be even more dynamics that push old buttons, bring out the worst in us and make it easy to sink into selfish living. God offers a better way. He has more for us than living as unbelieving blended couples do. He gave us the gift of His Spirit to lead us and guide us into truth. Remember, truth sets us free!

Consider the following:

> Jen and Mike had been married just 18 months when problems started to erupt. Her two children became a focal point of jealousy and bitterness for Mike's ex-wife and his only daughter. Before long both Jen and Mike were embroiled in a competition to protect their own turf. Steeped in pride and unwilling to let go, their marriage almost came to a devastating end. Realizing their love for each other, both Jen and Mike knew that something had to change. In the middle of their storm, both of them realized that their pride and stubbornness caused them to dig their heels in at all costs. They were each viewing their children from their first marriages as "his and hers" rather than "theirs," and in so doing they were unconsciously drawing lines and making two competing teams rather than one new family.[2]

23. What is it about Jen and Mike's situation that could eventually lead to a breakdown of their new marriage and family?

24. What can couples who come together and merge their lives and families do to lessen the presence of pride, protection and ownership?

25. Reread Romans 8:35,37 at the beginning of this session. What can make a spouse in a blended marriage feel separated from God's love?

26. Romans 8:37 says that in all these things we are more than conquerors. How could a couple apply this verse to walking through the new challenging territory of a blended marriage?

All relationships have times of struggle. Unfortunately in a blended marriage alliances make it easy to create sides. Our pride and personal family prejudice add to the pressure to create new teams. There comes a time when a commitment to the new relationship must be firmly reestablished. The firm stance of this new commitment calls for honesty, humility and large doses of hope. Then we will experience the power of God interceding on our behalf.

27. What are the things—attitudes, situations, feelings, etc.—that have put stress on your relationship? Make a list of these things and discuss with your spouse how you each can be honest, hopeful and humble in dealing with them together.

Be honest with your spouse about your feelings regarding disappointments with the challenges of your blending. If you need to confess to your spouse, do so, asking for prayer, cleansing and healing.

28. Share with your spouse the passage in this lesson that most spoke to you and how you plan to apply it to daily life.

This week memorize Philippians 4:6-8. As a couple, ask God to help you apply this verse and its principles to your life and marriage. If you do not already memorize meaningful Scripture, begin to make it a priority. Having God's Word in your mind can help, comfort and encourage you in the midst of a difficult situation.

Regularly set some time aside for each other. Take time right now to plan a date to spend time with one another without interruptions or distractions. What arrangements do you need to make to keep your date? Create a space and time for private conversation. Listen to your spouse. Don't judge, criticize or try to fix your spouse. Listen to the heart of the one to whom you have committed your heart.

Together confess to God your faults and inability to accept all challenges in your blended marriage. Ask for His help and for His grace and guidance. Throughout the week thank God for the hope you have in Christ. Remind your spouse of your commitment to him or her, and thank God daily that nothing separates you from His love and that in Christ you and your spouse are more than conquerors.

Notes

1. Edward Goodrick and John Kohlenberger, *The NIV Exhaustive Concordance* (Grand Rapids, MI: Zondervan Publishing House, 1990), p. 117, #2568.
2. This is a fictional account. Any resemblance to actual events or any people, living or dead, is purely coincidental.

living *with*
new challenges

"My grace is sufficient for you, for my power is made perfect in weakness."
Therefore I will boast all the more gladly about my weaknesses, so that Christ's power
may rest on me. That is why, for Christ's sake, I delight in weaknesses, in insults, in
hardships, in persecutions, in difficulties. For when I am weak, then I am strong.
2 Corinthians 12:9-10

Christians in a blended marriage often come to a crisis of belief, a fork in the road or at least an abrupt turning point when faced with the new, and sometimes tricky, challenges that come up in a remarriage. What once seemed like a new chance for a perfect love and a perfect family, as portrayed by *The Brady Bunch* TV series, ends up being far removed from the glitz and glamour of a Hollywood set. What once seemed like the perfect idea for the future can become the biggest challenge ever faced. Though some couples seemingly blend well from the start, most blend through trial, error and struggle. In a blended marriage the couple constantly needs to be flexible as individuals while reminding themselves not to give in to the temptation of isolation and selfishness—just doing things their own way.

Thankfully, Christ promises that He will never leave us or forsake us. In the midst of misunderstandings, rearranged family dynamics and the tug-of-war that goes on as relationships find their new settling place, the hope of Christ's presence with us is great news.

tilling the ground

There are many adjustments to be made as a new couple sifts through the rubble of the old life to build a new one. Often this sifting reveals problems. But when our focus shifts to the all-sufficient power of Christ within us, the sifting can bring about newfound freedom and a long-awaited peace. First, we have to be honest—stepping out of denial.

1. What challenges do you think are common to most blended marriages that are different from those of couples who are in a first marriage?

2. When compared to real life, what were some of the unrealistic aspects of *The Brady Bunch* TV series?

3. If a new reality show called *Blended Family Life* were created, what would some of the episodes or scenarios look like?

Blended Family Life is not filmed on a television set, and it is certainly not scripted by some crafty writers who can control how each episode will end. In this new reality every day is a new day and a new experience. Outside forces as well as past emotional and even financial baggage can threaten this marriage at every turn. At times those in a blended marriage feel the problems are too much to bear, too difficult to endure and too hard to live through. It takes humility or brokenness—and sometimes both—for a couple in a blended marriage to admit that they cannot adjust to some of these new dynamics without help. Through Christ and His strength, they cannot only survive, but they can also live in strength and power.

planting the seed

Learning to rely on God's strength is a biblical basic that most believers do not seek to learn about God's power until they are pressured by the realities of a not-so-perfect life. In a blended marriage, relying on God's strength and power to sustain us is essential to making it to the finish line. It is also important to see how relying on God makes us stronger than we were before.

The apostle Paul wrote frequently in his epistles about his weaknesses, hardships and being pressed hard on every side. Yet in spite of these hardships and trials, he was not crushed. His journey to humility and dependence on Jesus Christ was what made his life purposeful and effective in the end.

Could it be that the changes and challenges pressing in on you as you maneuver through your blended marriage will make your life more purposeful and effective in the end? Dependence on Christ begins when all your personal resources are depleted. If you are depleted—worn out from the challenges and confused by all the pieces of this puzzle called "the blended family"—you are actually in a good place. Now you have a choice: You can merely *go* through it or you can *grow* through it. If you choose to grow—baby step by baby step—you will be closer to your full maturity in Christ.

4. In 2 Corinthians 1:3-4, how did Paul describe the Lord?

The dictionary definitions for two of the words used in this passage are

- **Compassion:** A suffering with another; painful sympathy; a sensation of sorrow excited by the distress or misfortunes of another.[1]

- **Comfort:** To strengthen, to invigorate, to cheer or enliven. To strengthen the mind when depressed; to console; to give new vigor, to relieve from the depression of troubles.[2]

5. Think of one current challenge your marriage is experiencing. What comes to mind when you think of God the Father suffering with you in that challenge?

    What comes to mind when you realize that in Christ you can be relieved from the depression that often comes with troubles?

6. According to 2 Corinthians 1:3-7, what is the purpose of the comfort we receive in our challenges and sufferings?

7. In 2 Corinthians 1:8-10, Paul explained the pressure he faced while in Asia. How low did the pressure take him?

8. What was the purpose of Paul's sufferings according to 2 Corinthians 1:9?

    On what did Paul set his hope?

9. What would relying on God and not yourself look like in the real world of your blended marriage relationships with your children, stepchildren, in-laws, exes and spouse?

10. Read Psalm 18—a psalm of deliverance. David sang this psalm to the Lord when he was rescued from all his enemies and from Saul (see 2 Samuel 22:1-51). What verse from this psalm speaks to you most and why?

Psalm 18:2 describes several ways that God is able to deliver us from harm. List the characteristics of God in relation to His people during times of trouble.

Which characteristic do you most need in your present situation? Explain why.

It is clear that if we need protection, we are to look to God who is all-powerful. He is our rock. He cannot be moved and His faithfulness is not altered, despite the ever-changing circumstances of life. He is always a place of safety and refuge: a rock, a fortress, a shield, the strength of our salvation and our stronghold.

In her book *Blended Families*, author Maxine Marsolini quotes some alarming facts.

> More than half of Americans today have been, are now, or will eventually be in one or more step-situations during their lives. Why should this statistic alarm us? Because the stepfamily population is growing each year. The National Institute of Child Health and Human Development's newest demographic projections show that by the year 2000 more Americans will be living in stepfamilies than in nuclear family structures.
>
> The Institute enlisted Dr. James Bray to begin an extensive study of the stepfamily. In 1984 he and his group launched what became a nine-year study of families living with a stepparent, in particular a stepfather. One of the findings of his research was the high incidence of divorce in second marriages. Nearly 60 percent of these unions were not surviving. Many failed to make it past the first two years.[3]

Statistics like these remind us that conflicts in a remarriage are part of the uncharted territory. It also is a reminder that not only do we need the comfort and compassion of God, but we also need His strength and deliverance—for such a time as this.

Living in His Strength

There is a story in 2 Chronicles 20 about King Jehoshaphat and how he handled the news of pending trouble. In this chapter we can find many things that will help us stay strong no matter how many difficult situations, obstacles or seeming enemies we face.

11. In 2 Chronicles 20:1-3, what threat was Jehoshaphat facing, what was his immediate reaction and how did he respond to the threat?

12. Describe a time in your life when it felt like an enemy army was coming against you. What was your immediate reaction and how did you respond to the threat of danger or discomfort?

In this passage we can see three significant things:

1. Jehoshaphat was informed in advance.
2. Jehoshaphat was immediately alarmed by what he knew to be coming.
3. Jehoshaphat made the decision to seek the Lord.

Those of us in a blended marriage have been informed in advance by facts and statistics that life will sometimes be hard, even seemingly impossible, to endure. Jesus has also warned us that we would have troubles in this life (see John 16:33). This is alarming in our "I just want to be happy" culture. Our culture has conditioned us to watch out for number one and to follow our own heart. Yet 2 Chronicles 20 teaches that when we are alarmed by life's challenges, we need to focus on the Lord and seek His help.

13. What does Jeremiah 17:9 say about the human heart?

It is important to remember that God is always working in us at the heart level. Though the world around us may seem out of control and our circumstances may seem crazy, God is always at work. His main concern is our spiritual maturity and our walk of faith. If our challenges take us to a place of total dependence on God, then they have accomplished the greatest purpose of all.

14. How does Jeremiah 17:5-8 relate to the challenges of blending a bro-ken family?

Living Through the Challenges

A blended marriage is full of change. We can see how to handle change by looking again at King Jehoshaphat. There are three characteristics of his rela-tionship with God that will also benefit us (see 2 Chronicles 20:1-12):

- **Confession:** Lord, I am alarmed at how difficult this new life is!
- **Praise:** Lord, I honor You with my present life and circum-stances. Power and might are in Your hands; You know what it will take to bring us together!
- **Humility:** We don't know what to do with this situation, but our eyes are on You.

15. What did God promise Jehoshaphat in 2 Chronicles 20:15-17?

What instructions did He give to the king and the people that relate directly to a difficult situation—a vast army?

A vast army can be anything that is too big for us to handle. We all face such battles from time to time. Statistics about the difficulties of blending a family could have us cower in fear for the survival of our blended marriage. But God says the battle is not ours, it's His. Notice that He told Jehoshaphat *twice* to not be afraid or discouraged.

16. What do you think "take up your positions and stand firm" (2 Chronicles 20:17) means in an everyday blended marriage?

17. Describe a time when you realized that you were in a situation that was beyond your ability to handle. What did you learn from this situation?

Three clear-cut actions of Jehoshaphat should serve as an example in any type of battle:

1. Take up your position.
2. Stand firm.
3. See the deliverance of the Lord.

Take Up Your Position

Ephesians 2:1-10 describes our position in Christ.

18. According to Ephesians 2:4-6, what did Christ do for us?

How should being in this position give us courage to face anything?

What parallels exist between your blended relationship and what Christ did for you as described in Ephesians 2:4-6?

Stand Firm

19. Ephesians 6:10-14 speaks of standing firm against the devil's schemes. What specific things can you identify as potential schemes against your blended family?

20. What does 1 Peter 5:8-9 say about your enemy and what your response should be?

It's much easier to think that a person is our enemy—and people certainly do things to attack and hurt us. But part of standing firm is realizing who the real enemy is. The devil's scheme is to destroy your new family, rob you of your peace and integrity, and use every opportunity to negatively affect your children.

21. John 10:10-11 compares the differences between a thief and a shepherd. What does the thief come to do? What has the "thief" tried to steal from your marriage?

What does the shepherd come to do? How have you experienced this in your relationship?

See the Deliverance of the Lord

22. What does Hebrews 2:14-18 say regarding God's ability to deliver you from present troubles?

God's most powerful description of Himself is recorded in Exodus 3:14 when He says, "I AM WHO I AM." He is everything that is perfect, excellent and holy. He was from the beginning and will be until the end. He is

- EVERYTHING you will ever need for comfort when in the battle zone;
- EVERYTHING you will ever need when seeking guidance, direction and counsel;
- EVERYTHING you will ever need when called to love children and family who aren't your own;
- EVERYTHING you will ever need when you must turn the other cheek;
- EVERYTHING you will ever need to rise above the natural tendencies of the flesh nature in order to walk in the Spirit in this new marriage and its dynamics.

 watering the hope

Consider the following:

Annie took to crying in the shower. Only three months into this new marriage and her dream life had already become a nightmare. Jim's children didn't like her; his ex-wife claimed that Annie wasn't good for their three children and constantly undermined any good thing she had accomplished with her stepchildren; and her new in-laws had trust issues and an overprotective spirit toward their son and his children. Never having been a mother before, she had hoped to be Super Stepmom, not Wicked Stepmother. As she cried uncontrollably in the shower—where no one could hear—she was certain that she had made the biggest mistake of her life.

It seemed to Annie that she was the one who had to continually forgo her needs, feelings or desires to keep the peace. She had quickly learned her need to confess each hardship to the Lord as it occurred. She also learned that she had to trust in God's power and might, not her own. After all, she had run out of her own strength a long time ago! For the first time in her life she longed, really longed, to know God as the Father of compassion and the source of all comfort—but comfort seemed elusive.

In the first three years of marriage, Annie had considered leaving on five occasions; she couldn't stand the pain any longer. Then that still, small voice in her soul reminded her not only of her commitment and covenant with God and to Jim but also of the greater good that such hard times would later produce in her spiritually. But she didn't know if she could stand firm and survive the hardships piled one on top of another.[4]

23. To what in Annie and Jim's situation can you relate?

24. What is a person in a remarriage to do when everyone seems unfairly aligned against him or her?

25. What could Jim do that would be more supportive of Annie and their situation?

What practical steps could Annie take to alleviate as much stress and pain as possible?

26. Consider the key verse for this session, 2 Corinthians 12:9-10, once again. What is made perfect in our times of weakness and what are we to do in our weaknesses?

"Delight" means "to take great pleasure in" or "to rejoice."[5] Why do you think the apostle Paul was able to say that he could "delight in weaknesses, in insults, in hardships, in persecutions, in difficulties"?

There is no mistaking that every blended marriage faces challenges. It is also true that within these challenges we can be changed for the better, experience the power of Christ resting on us and be blessed with comfort that will in turn comfort others and give them hope. "One thing for sure—blending doesn't just happen. We purposely journey into it. And it takes years."[6]

 harvesting the fruit

Every marriage encounters challenges and hardships. Whether it's the first time around or a remarriage, centering your marriage on a relationship with Jesus Christ will give you hope and strength in the tough times.

27. Evaluate the needs in your relationship today. What challenges are you up against that would require you to take up your position, stand firm and see the deliverance of the Lord? Communicate with your mate about these challenges.

28. Together make a list of actions you could each take to lighten the other's load, showing support for one another within your new family situation.

Your marriage is the most important relationship and the foundation of the entire family. Plan a date with your spouse at least once a week. Remember that the date is not the time to discuss your challenges. Instead, enjoy each other, embrace your love and build your relationship. Your problems will be waiting for you when you return; tomorrow is another day to experience Christ's being everything you need!

Also schedule some alone time in which the two of you can prayerfully discuss the challenges you are encountering in blending your family. This should be a regularly planned time, ideally once each day, but at least two to three times each week.

Notes

1. *An American Dictionary of the English Language*, 15th ed., s.v. "compassion."
2. Ibid., s.v. "comfort."
3. Maxine Marsolini, *Blended Families* (Chicago, IL: Moody Press, 2000), p. 10.
4. This is a fictional account. Any resemblance to actual events or any people, living or dead, is purely coincidental.
5. *An American Dictionary of the English Language*, s.v. "delight."
6. Marsolini, *Blended Families*, p. 14.

living *with*
new relationships

God is love. Whoever lives in love lives in God, and God in him.
1 John 4:16

Three issues that often wedge themselves between marriage partners in a blended marriage are finances, ex-spouses and the children. Because a blended marriage is built on the broken bedrock of past relationships, things can get rocky real quick. Remnants of previous responsibilities and lingering unspoken hurts can fuel some nasty situations. Learning a new language of love, one that puts others first, may prove to be the hardest challenge in the family dynamics of a blended marriage.

God calls us to love one another, but we often don't relate the command to everyday life. We add conditions to His command, convincing ourselves that there is a menu of options dependent on our present circumstances or the dynamics of our current relationships. It would be easy to learn to live in God's love if we were alone on a mountaintop or tucked away in a cave. There in the quietness and peace of not having to deal with other people, we could think about God's love in theory but not have to put it into practice. In this place of seclusion, we could love everybody and everything. Nothing would stop us: no disappointments, no disagreements, no conflicts. But add up all the complex relationships in a blended marriage—in-laws, out-laws, exes and children: yours, mine and ours—and you have the potential for a real war on your hands. And it all starts with saying, "I do."

More and more people who remarry find themselves with an instant family, saying "I do" to more than just a spouse—there are the kids, the in-laws, the out-laws (former in-laws) the exes and the family pets as well. Nearly two out of three remarriages today involve children from a previous marriage, and many newly married couples find that the word "stepfamily" brings more than they bargained for.[1]

1. What do you think is the single most debated issue between husband and wife in a blended marriage?

2. When called to love children that are not their own, do you think most people adjust naturally or have internal struggles? Why?

3. Of the three challenges—finances, ex-spouses and the children—which is the most challenging for you as a married couple today? Why?

Interestingly, all three areas have something to do with the future security of the children. If there are children in your blended mix, their lives and hearts are important to God. As Christian adults, we cannot teach them about the love of Jesus if we live in bitterness and unforgiveness toward their other parent. We also cannot play a protective role in their lives if we are not part of their financial provision. Far too often, bitterness and unforgiveness toward the ex-spouse fuel the climate in blended family relations.

When Christians find themselves in a remarriage, they might become concerned about the spiritual legacy that has seemingly been robbed from their family tree. What once was meant to be a godly heritage for the next generation now appears to be a broken limb on a tree that has branches shooting out in every direction.

Take heart, there is still a legacy to leave. It might not be the original legacy that you dreamed of but a legacy nonetheless. With the help of God's grace and the work of His Spirit, we can still leave a legacy of grace, love and forgiveness. God has the power to accomplish this, but He calls us to cooperate with Him in the kingdom work of loving when it seems the hardest thing to do.

4. According to 1 Corinthians 13, what are the characteristics of love?

There are many kinds of love, including romantic, brotherly and familial love. In this passage the Greek word *agape*, denoting affection, good will, benevolence and unconditional love, is translated "love." It represents the love of God for His people.[2]

5. Which characteristics of love as stated in 1 Corinthians 13 are a particular challenge to express in a blended marriage?

Which characteristic is being lived out in your family? Which is the one your family most needs to experience?

6. Sometimes we don't feel like there is an ounce of love or benevolence left in us for the people who continually disrupt the peace of our homes. What do 1 John 4:16 and Romans 5:5 tell us about God's love?

Since God has poured His love into our hearts by the Holy Spirit, how should this have an impact on how we as Christians in blended families treat one another?

7. According to Romans 13:10, what is a statement of love and how can this apply to a stepchild? To an ex-spouse, in-law or out-law?

8. Second Timothy 2:22 instructs us to "pursue righteousness, faith, love and peace." What would this look like in our relationships?

Pursuing love often requires a change in lifestyle. It calls for denial of self for the sake of obedience to the greater call of Christ.

9. Explore how 1 John 4:7-12 gives a foundation for how we are to relate to others. What does verse 12 say will be complete in us when we chase after love?

Note that these verses say Christ came into the world that *we might live through Him*. Christian agape love is not a product of our emotions or feelings; it does not always correspond with our natural inclinations, nor does it allow us to pick and choose who we will love or not love. God's love in us gives us the ability to seek the best for others. The love of God has been placed in our hearts, and it is only by His power that we can live out that love in our lives.

New Foundations

10. What does Matthew 7:24-27 tells us about building a life foundation?

11. According to Matthew 22:37-40, what should be the foundation of our life in Christ?

12. Some people seem impossible to love. What do the following verses tell us about the "impossible": Matthew 17:20; Luke 1:37; 18:27; Hebrews 11:6?

13. A new heart foundation is possible too. What does Ezekiel 36:26-27 tell us about a new heart?

After reading these verses do you still think it is impossible to love some of the new people in your life? What about when you are worn out and wounded by a stepchild's behavior? What about when you are continually taken to court by a relentless ex-spouse? What about the financial drain of supporting two families? What about the times your own spouse behaves unfairly toward your child? Impossible? No, your problems and impossibilities are now God's possibilities, and He is the key to creating healthy relationships in your blended family.

New Attitudes

14. Colossians 3:1-17 describes rules for holy living. How do these verses relate to living with difficult relationships?

15. Grievances are part of life in this new family. What does Colossians 3:13 say we are to do in these cases?

16. No matter how disjointed or convoluted your blended family may seem, it is still a family unit. What does Colossians 3:15-16 say about living as a unit?

The stepfamily is not a nuclear family, but it is a family nonetheless. Certain realities are a normal part of the blending process:

- Expect outside influences to intrude.
- Expect children to feel torn between both parents.
- Be prepared for change.
- Be willing to make sacrifices for the common good.
- Understand that your expectations will most likely have to be adjusted.
- Define love as commitment, not merely feelings.
- Remember that effective blending doesn't happen overnight.
- Realize that sometimes blending doesn't go smoothly.
- Be committed to the covenant of your marriage regardless of circumstances.

New Choices

17. What did Jesus teach in Luke 6:27-36?

What might be some results—both good and bad—of loving someone as Jesus commands us to do in this passage?

Oftentimes there is someone in the new relational mix that is difficult to love. That person might be a continual source of heartache for you and your family. Christ taught that even though unbelievers love those who love them, His followers are to love regardless of whether that love is returned.

18. How might Matthew 25:40 relate to loving someone else's child or ex?

19. What does Colossians 3:21 say about the way we treat our children—yours, mine or ours?

20. Ephesians 6:2-3 tells us how we are to treat our parents. What should we be teaching our children about their "other family"?

Let's be honest. It might be easy to be unfair or more critical of our stepchildren because of differences in personality and their environment. Yet as believers we are to raise the standard in our lives and choose to follow the example of Christ. Remember, without love we are a clanging bell (see 1 Corinthians 13:1)!

watering the hope

Consider Larry and Marie's story.

Larry loved when his children came for the weekend. In his excitement of preparing for their visit, he came to life—planning outings, special events and anything else that would make their time together special. But on the weekends they weren't scheduled to visit, he was usually away from home honing his golf game. Marie's children believed that they weren't important enough for special events or for Larry's time. His heart seemed to be reserved only for his own children. Just looking and longing for love, the hole in the hearts of Marie's children grew wider and deeper through the years. By the time they were in their teens, they just checked out of the family altogether. Marie was filled with resentment. Who was this man who served in ministries at church but never even tried to love her children—his stepchildren?

Marie also had to cope with intrusive and hateful telephone calls from her stepchildren's biological mother. The woman told her children that Marie would never love them as much as she loved them because they could never be Marie's blood relations. She was constantly making up bizarre stories that put Marie in a bad light with her stepchildren The children grew to hate Marie, making her into the wicked stepmother. Larry, feeling torn between his new wife and his own children, tried to patch up the situation, but it only grew worse. Larry and Marie realized that the foundation of their new family was on shaky ground, and that they had quit communicating because of the disappointment and hurt.[3]

21. How does Philippians 4:11-13 relate to difficult relationships?

Philippians 4:13 is a promise for even the most difficult of situations. What is this promise and how can we hold on to it?

22. What does Romans 12:9-21 say about dealing with difficult people?

How can someone relate to an intrusive ex-spouse or bitter child while still maintaining the integrity of his or her Christian walk?

Remember, children learn by what is modeled before them. Does your interaction with your stepchild or your spouse's ex reflect the love of God? As you are a vessel of God's love to that child, you show him or her the truth of God's love. As you show God's love to an ex-spouse, you may be a catalyst for peace in both families.

harvesting the fruit

Every blended family will have struggles as they adjust to outside influences and pressures, and to stepchildren and exes—even to grandparents from both sides of the family. It is only through our commitment to the Lord and to one another that we will be able to see it through to the end. This side of heaven, no family is perfect; but as we seek to live out Christ's love in our lives, we can leave a legacy of love for our families.

23. Deuteronomy 6:6-7 and Psalm 78:6 speak to us about the legacy we leave. How does this notion of legacy relate to your blended family today?

In what legacy have you invested so far?

What could you do to improve your family's legacy?

24. Take inventory of the needs of your children. Together with your spouse evaluate how your children are doing. Discuss what problems need to be addressed and how the legacy of love, grace and forgiveness can begin healing their hearts from the brokenness that has affected all of your lives.

List one specific action that each of you can take to build a stronger relationship with each child in your family.

25. How are the exes affecting your relationship?

List specific actions that you can take to do your part "as far as it depends on you, [to] live at peace with everyone" (Romans 12:18).

Perhaps the following 10 rules for confident stepparenting might help as you deal with the realities of blending relationships in your family:

1. Be proud of the role you are assuming.
2. Be realistic. Check all rosy expectations at the door.
3. Love your spouse.
4. Be flexible.
5. Respect yourself, so the children will be free to respect you.
6. Remember that you are not a replacement. You are an original, crafted and equipped by God to meet whatever comes your way.
7. Take time to adjust, to listen, to pray, to play.
8. Let go of destructive anger.
9. Reach out for help when you need it
10. Watch for invisible, simple blessings.[4]

26. Which action or attitude in this list would be most helpful in your present situation and how can you implement it?

Commit to your spouse the importance of adjusting expectations, of honoring each other by honoring one another's children, and of making every effort to seek peace in all extended relationships. Talk about what that would look like and why that could be uncomfortable at first. Together decide to align your lives, your minds and your hearts to the truth in God's Word regarding how you treat other people. Memorize specific verses from Romans 12:9-21 that will help in specific situations with which you are dealing right now.

Notes

1. Angela Elwell Hunt, *Loving Someone Else's Child* (Wheaton, IL: Tyndale House Publishers, 1992), p. 23.
2. *Thayer's Greek Lexicon*. 4th ed. CD-ROM, version 3.1, BibleSoft.
3. This is a fictional account. Any resemblance to actual events or any people, living or dead, is purely coincidental.
4. Hunt, *Loving Someone Else's Child*, p. 223.

living with new hope

May the God of hope fill you with all joy and peace as you trust in him,
so that you may overflow with hope by the power of the Holy Spirit.
Romans 15:13

Statistics are clear: Most remarriages struggle to survive.[1] However, in Christ
we can be more than a statistic—we can have hope. The things that threaten
the peace and stability of a blended marriage can be viewed with hope and
with faith in God, who has started a good work in us and will most certainly see it to completion (see Philippians 1:6).

When hope wanes, we can reflect on how God has met our needs in the
past. Remembering how we have weathered the storms of past relationships,
we can cling to His promises of a hope-filled future (see Jeremiah 29:11). Also
what we have learned from past experiences can be applied for the good of
our present relationships.

tilling the ground

Having an eternal focus is a key ingredient in changing our attitudes amid the dynamics of blended family living. The focus must be off other people, outside circumstances and relentless challenges, and turned toward Jesus and our future with Him. The new cry of the heart should be "Lord, change me!" Though change is hard, it is at the same time full of personal growth and the fulfillment of knowing that through it all Christ is being formed in you.

1. How many blended marriages do you know that have become a statistic of failure? What do you believe was a key ingredient in the failure of those relationships?

2. What steps can couples in blended marriages take to insure that their marriage will not be another statistical failure?

3. How does a person change his or her focus or attitude?

   Why is attitude so important to the quality of life?

4. What have you learned from your past relationships that can give you hope for the future of your present relationship?

Whether you are committing to loving a stepchild, accepting an ex-spouse or balancing a joint checking account, you must make sure to keep your marriage strong. Initially in a stepfamily it may be difficult for the husband and wife to solidify their relationship—it is overshadowed by so many outside forces. The spouse may feel like an intruder in the family unit, but the bond of the husband and wife must be strong if the family is to stay together.

Emily Visher, a therapist in Palo Alto, California, says "It's hard to have a honeymoon in the middle of a crowd, but you really need to nourish the couple relationship."[2] If the couple loses hope, the entire family fails. A remarriage succeeds best when there is ample time for being a couple, strengthening the covenant of marriage and growing as one in Christ.

planting the seed

There are two ways of approaching life in a blended marriage: as victims or as victors. For many, victim thinking can steal the hope, joy and gratitude from what God has provided in this new mate and new family. Lost expectations from days gone by can make the glass seem half empty when in actuality it can be filled by God Himself each day. Ungratefulness or negativity can blind you to the good and completely alter your focus.

5. What does Galatians 5:1 say about living outside God's best? How can having an out-of-focus life become "a yoke of slavery"?

Christ set us free for a very distinct purpose. He intended for us to live as those who were freed from the bondage and slavery of selfishness and sin.

6. How can Galatians 5:7-10 be related to blended family dynamics?

Just as a tiny spark can start a raging fire, a misspoken word or a selfish attitude may start a raging argument in a tense situation. When something or someone cuts off the good work of God in our midst, remember that the temptation to go back to our old ways of hopelessness comes from our enemy, the devil.

7. Galatians 5:13-15 reminds us of our freedom in Christ. What kinds of blended family situations can trip us up, destroying our freedom?

What does Galatians 5:15 say regarding our interaction with others?

How can we live out the command of Galatians 5:16?

8. How are the acts of the flesh nature as listed in Galatians 5:19-21 related to the attitudes and actions often represented in blended family dynamics?

9. In contrast, what are the fruit, or evidences, of the Spirit as listed in Galatians 5:22-23?

In what ways have you experienced the effects of the fruit of the Spirit in your own family situation?

Which fruit is the most difficult for you to personally apply? Why?

10. Galatians 5:25 is a key verse reminding us to stay in step with the Holy Spirit. What is it saying to you regarding your blended marriage relationship?

There is a saying, Feed the Spirit—starve the flesh. What you feed will be well nourished and will grow; what is left unfed will shrivel up and die. Choices produce changes.

Jesus was an encourager. Everywhere He went, He offered hope to the hurting and downcast. He's the God of the second, third and fourth chance—His mercies are new every morning (see Lamentations 3:23).

Choosing to Hope

11. Lamentations 3:18-24 describes the author's many afflictions and yet he still has hope. What practical encouragement is found in these verses?

12. How might Hebrews 3:13 apply to daily life in a blended marriage?

13. In John 8:3-11 we can learn the value of compassion and a gentle word as we see Jesus interact with sinful human nature. Since Jesus—who never sinned—didn't throw stones, how can we apply this same attitude in our own interactions with others?

Sadly, encouragement is one ingredient often missing in the varied relationships of a blended family. As family battle lines are drawn, we often feel like it's us against them rather than a family that is learning to love one another. In any family, love must be learned; but in a stepfamily, love usually does not come naturally—it requires concentrated effort. In Christ the unnatural comes to life with His supernatural touch.

Choosing to Stay

Every marriage—whether the original dream or a new chance at love—can get out of focus. First marriages have struggles just as blended marriages do, yet two people in a remarriage who have come together after the loss of love may become frustrated more readily and be more easily tempted to throw in the towel sooner. Divorce should not be an option. A commitment to stay even through the most difficult of adjustments will give the other partner the feeling of safety to learn and grow in this new family.

14. How does Matthew 12:25 (compare Mark 3:25 and Luke 11:17) relate to a troubled marriage relationship?

15. How can knowing that your spouse is committed to staying in your marriage strengthen your relationship?

Psalm 127:1 speaks directly to the foundation of any family, but a blended family may have more opportunities for the foundation to develop stress fractures and begin to crumble. If the Lord is not your firm foundation, your home is built on shaky ground. You and your spouse need to confirm that you are in this relationship for the long haul and commit that you will rely on the Lord for the strength to stay.

Choosing to Connect

If the Lord is going to build anything of lasting value in our life, we must first be connected to Him. Our connection with Him fosters love for others.

16. John 15:4 tells us to do something that requires daily choice. What must we do to "remain in" Christ?

17. What is the promise of John 15:5? How have you experienced this promise in your relationship?

18. According to John 15:7-8, what is the ultimate result of remaining connected to the Lord?

Daily prayer and Scripture reading are often overlooked in the day-to-day busyness of our lives—that is, until there is a crisis. Connecting daily with the Lord is extremely important if we are to meet the demands of each day. Just as we need food to fuel our bodies, we need spiritual nourishment to fuel our souls. We must realize the power of asking God for His help, guidance and grace to deal with all that life throws at us. He is honored, willing to respond and ultimately glorified through our connection to the power source—His Spirit.

Choosing Godly Wisdom

As we stay connected to God through prayer and reading His Word, we will gain knowledge and wisdom that can help us as we blend our family.

19. How does Proverbs 24:3-4 relate to the blended family?

How can knowledge fill a home with rare and beautiful treasures?

What would those treasures be?

20. What does Proverbs 24:14 say about hope?

21. Proverbs 8:10-11 and 9:10-11 instruct that we have a choice. How does this relate to your situation?

22. How can Jeremiah 29:11-13 be a source of hope during difficult times?

Every day we make choices. Some are as simple as choosing what clothes to wear or what to fix for dinner. But others have greater consequences. Choosing to place hope in our loving heavenly Father, to commit to staying with our spouse for better and for worse, to daily connect with the Lord through prayer and His Word, and to rely on His wisdom and grow in our knowledge of Him will have eternal results.

 watering the hope

Consider the James and Donna's story.

James and Donna have been married a little over a year. They are both in their third marriage. Donna's 17-year-old son, Nick, the apple of her eye, lives with them. Nick only sees his birth father a few times a year because he lives over 2,000 miles away. James has no children of his own. The thought of being a stepparent was exciting to James. Both James and Nick have common interests in sports and the outdoors, but Nick is a busy high school senior, which makes it difficult for the two of them to spend time together.

Nick at times seems to be hungry for a relationship with James, but lately he has been more and more antagonistic. Whenever there is a big blowup between Nick and James, Donna feels the need to step in and protect Nick. Then James and Donna end up in a heated argument. Sometimes the blowups are over normal teenage issues as Nick strains to be an adult and yet still acts like a kid. The really serious blowups often seem to be directly related to those times when Nick's father has disappointed Nick. The stress is beginning to wear on James, and he has begun to wonder if this marriage is worth the pain it is causing. James has decided to seek counseling.

James confides his frustrations to his counselor. "I don't feel like I'm number one to Donna," he says with frustration. "I feel Nick is. I'm her husband, so I'm supposed to be her priority."

"To begin with," the counselor says, "you need to understand that Donna and her son have had a relationship for 17 years. You have only been in their lives for a short time. It won't pay for you to covet the bond they have as mother and son. What difference does it make if you are 100 percent right—if you win the battle and lose the war? Understand the source of most of your conflicts with Nick; he may be projecting his anger at his own father on to you. Nick needs a stepdad and a home that are a refuge for him: someone he can count on to be there for him, a place where he can express his feelings honestly and still feel loved."[3]

23. What could James do to strengthen his relationship with Nick? With Donna?

Where do you see hope in their situation?

24. What about Donna and James's situation can you relate to?

25. Proverbs 4:23 tells us to guard our hearts above all else, for out of our hearts the substance of our lives flows. How can a person guard his or her heart against unrealistic expectations, unmet needs or undeserved attacks?

26. What does Proverbs 4:25-27 tell us to do that can be applied daily in a blended family?

27. Jeremiah 31:3-4 has a message of God's love that is pertinent for those in a blended marriage. What hope do you find in this passage?

28. What gives you the most hope for your relationship?

   What presently makes you feel the most hopeless?

29. What Scripture passage(s) from this session encouraged hope in you? Why?

   What have you learned from your past relationship(s) that has actually helped—even given you hope—in your present relationship?

   Memorize specific Scriptures that have spoken to you in this session. That way God's Word will be an encouragement for you when you most need it.

30. Share with your spouse your commitment to stay together for better and for worse. How will you put this commitment into action? List one action that you personally will take this week to communicate commitment to your spouse.

31. Strengthen your commitment to connect to Christ for help, hope and healing. What is one specific action that you can take as a couple to strengthen your commitment to Christ?

As you share your answers with your spouse, be honest about the areas you are struggling with and take time to pray for one another now and throughout the coming weeks. Share with each other what encourages hope in you and express your thanks to God for His love and encouragement in your life together. In those areas in which you struggle, choose one action that you can take now to strengthen your relationship with one another. As you begin to see results, praise the Lord for His faithfulness.

Commit to doing weekly, monthly and yearly checkups of your relationships with each other and with God. Formulate new action plans as previous struggles are rectified.

Notes
1. Maxine Marsolini, *Blended Families* (Chicago, IL: Moody Press, 2000), p. 10.
2. Emily Visher, quoted in Amanda Morgan, "Happy Stepfamilies: What Are They Doing Right?" *Redbook*, (May 1989), p. 129.
3. This is a fictional account. Any resemblance to actual events or any people, living or dead, is purely coincidental.

leader's discussion guide

General Guidelines

1. If at all possible, the group should be led by a married couple in a blended marriage. This does not mean that both spouses need to be leading the discussions; perhaps one spouse is better at facilitating discussions while the other is better at relationship building or organization—but the leader couple should share responsibilities wherever possible.

2. At the first meeting, be sure to lay down the ground rules for discussions, stressing that following these rules will help everyone feel comfortable during discussion times.

   a. No one should share anything of a personal or potentially embarrassing nature without first asking his or her spouse's permission.

   b. Too much personal information regarding details of court cases, custody battles or ex-spouses should be discouraged as it can be dishonoring to those involved.

   c. Whatever is discussed in the group meeting is to be held in strictest confidence among group members only.

   d. Allow everyone in the group to participate. However, as a leader, don't force anyone to answer a question if he or she is reluctant. Be sensitive to the different personalities and communication styles among your group members.

3. Fellowship time is very important in building small-group relationships. Providing beverages and/or light refreshments either before or

after each session will encourage a time of informal fellowship.

4. Most people live very busy lives; respect the time of your group members by beginning and ending meetings on time.

How to Use the Material

1. Each session has more than enough material to cover in a 45-minute teaching period. You will probably not have time to discuss every single question in each session, so prepare for each meeting by selecting questions you feel are most important to address for your group; discuss other questions as time permits. Be sure to save the last 10 minutes of your meeting time for each couple to interact individually and to pray together before adjourning.

   Optional Eight-Session Plan—You can easily divide each session into two parts if you'd like to cover all of the material presented in each session. Each section of the session has enough questions to divide in half, and the Bible study sections (Planting the Seed) are divided into two or three sections that can be taught in separate sessions.

2. Each spouse should have his or her own copy of the book in order to personally answer the questions. The general plan of this study is that the couples complete the questions at home during the week and then bring their books to the meeting to share what they have learned during the week.

   However, the reality of leading small groups in this day and age is that some members will find it difficult to do the homework. If you find that to be the case with your group, consider adjusting the lessons and having members complete the study during your meeting time as you guide them through the lesson. If you use this method, be sure to encourage members to share their individual answers with their spouse during the week—perhaps on a date night.

Session One | Living the Unexpected

Before the Meeting

1. Gather materials for making name tags. Also gather pens or pencils, 3x5-inch index cards and Bibles.
2. Make photocopies of the Prayer Request Form (found in *The Focus on the Family Marriage Ministry Guide*, "Reproducible Forms" section), or provide index cards for recording requests.
3. Read through your own answers and mark the ones that you especially want to have the group discuss. Also highlight key verses you feel are appropriate to share.
4. Prepare slips of paper with the references for the verses that you will want someone to read aloud during the session. Distribute these slips as group members arrive, but be sensitive to those who are uncomfortable reading aloud or who might not be familiar with the Bible.

Ice Breakers

1. If this is the first meeting for this couples group, have everyone introduce themselves and tell the group a brief summary of how they met their spouse, how long they have been married and one interesting fact about their spouse. Be sure to remind them not to reveal anything that their spouse would be uncomfortable sharing about him- or herself.
2. Use one of the following ice breakers to help members become better acquainted:
   a. **Option 1**—Ask each couple to share the funniest thing that happened at their wedding.
   b. **Option 2**—Ask each couple to share the biggest surprise they've discovered about blending their family.
3. Begin with prayer.

Discussion

1. **Tilling the Ground**—The purpose of this section is to get the group involved in a discussion of the topic at hand. These questions will usually be of a lighter, more generic tone. Invite volunteers to share their answers to these questions.

2. **Planting the Seed**—This section is the Bible study and is intended to lay out the biblical concepts for the session. Be sure to have the verses that you feel are key read aloud during this time for discussion. You do not need to discuss every question. You can skip any questions of a personal nature, but encourage couples to answer these during the Harvesting the Fruit time with their spouse.

3. **Watering the Hope**—The case study and questions in this section will help members bring the Bible study into the realities of their own blended family. Don't neglect this part of the study, as it brings the whole lesson into the here and now, applying God's Word to daily life.

   Have each couple pair up with another couple to read the case study and discuss the questions.

4. **Harvesting the Fruit**—This section is meant to help each couple apply the lesson to their own marriage and can be handled in several ways.

   a. Allow couples one-on-one time to interact at the end of the meeting. This would require time for them to be alone, with enough space between couples to allow for private conversation.

      If couples have already answered the questions individually, now would be the time to share their answers. Set a time limit, emphasizing that their discussions can be continued at home if they are not able to answer all of the questions in the time allotted.

      If couples have not answered the questions before the meeting, have them answer the questions together now. This works best when there is time after the meeting for the couples to stay until they have completed their discussion and will require that the leaders stay until the last couple has finished.

   b. Instruct couples to discuss this section at home during the week after the meeting. This will give them quiet, private time to deal with any issues that might come up and to spend all the time needed to complete the discussion. You will want to follow up at the next meeting to hold couples accountable for completing this part of the lesson.

c. At times it might be advantageous to pair up two couples to discuss these questions. This would also help build accountability into the study.

Allow time for the individual couples to meet together to complete this section of the questions.

5. **Close in Prayer**—An important part of any small-group relationship is the time spent in prayer for one another. This may be accomplished in a number of ways.

a. Have couples write out their specific prayer requests on the Prayer Request Forms (or index cards). These requests may then be shared with the whole group or traded with another couple as prayer partners for the week. If requests are shared with the whole group, pray as a group before adjourning the meeting; if requests are traded, allow time for the prayer-partner couples to pray together.

b. Gather the whole group together and lead couples in guided prayer.

c. Have individual couples pray together.

d. Split the members into two groups by gender. Have them pray over their marriages, asking God to reveal any issues that they need to work on in their blended family.

After the Meeting

1. **Evaluate**—Spend time evaluating the meeting's effectiveness (see *The Focus on the Family Marriage Ministry Guide*, "Reproducible Forms" section).

2. **Encourage**—During the week, try to contact each couple (through phone calls, notes of encouragement, e-mails or instant messages) and welcome them to the group. Make yourself available to answer any questions or concerns they may have and generally get to know them. This contact might best be done by the husband-leader contacting the men and the wife-leader contacting the women.

3. **Equip**—Complete the Bible study, even if you have previously gone through this study together.

4. **Pray**—Prayerfully prepare for the next meeting, praying for each couple and your own preparation. Discuss with the Lord any apprehension,

excitement or anything else that is on your mind regarding your Bible study material and/or the group members. If you feel inadequate or unprepared, ask for strength and insight. If you feel tired or burdened, ask for God's light yoke. Whatever it is you need, ask God for it. He will provide!

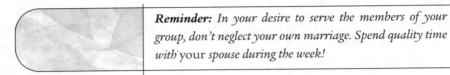

Reminder: *In your desire to serve the members of your group, don't neglect your own marriage. Spend quality time with your spouse during the week!*

Session Two | Living with New Challenges

Before the Meeting

1. Gather materials for making name tags. Also gather pens or pencils, 3x5-inch index cards and Bibles.
2. Make photocopies of the Prayer Request Form, or provide index cards for recording requests.
3. Read through your own answers and mark the ones that you especially want to have the group discuss. Also highlight key verses you feel are appropriate to share.
4. Prepare slips of paper with the references for the verses that you will want someone to read aloud during the session. Distribute these slips as group members arrive, but be sensitive to those who are uncomfortable reading aloud or who might not be familiar with the Bible.

Ice Breakers

1. Greet members as they arrive and give them a Prayer Request Form or index card to record prayer requests.
2. Invite couples to share how they applied what they learned in last week's session to their relationship.
3. Ask volunteers to share one praise or good thing that happened during the past week. This is an opportunity for those who might not always see the good in things to learn how to express gratitude and thanksgiving to God no matter what the circumstance.
4. Begin with prayer.

Discussion

1. **Tilling the Ground**—Invite volunteers to share what challenges they think are probably the most common in blended marriages but not an issue in first marriages. Discuss the answers to the rest of the questions as time allows.

2. **Planting the Seed**—Form groups of four to discuss the questions in this section.
3. **Watering the Hope**—Allow small groups to continue the discussion and have them share their answers to question 25 with the whole group.
4. **Harvesting the Fruit**—Invite couples to share their answers with their spouse.
5. **Close in Prayer**—Have couples pray together. As couples leave, have each one select an index card with another couple's prayer request. Ask them to pray for the couple in the coming week and contact them via phone, e-mail or personal note.

After the Meeting

1. **Evaluate**—Spend time evaluating the meeting's effectiveness.
2. **Encourage**—Contact each couple during the week and see how they are doing. Ask if they have had a date with their spouse and if they have a challenge for which they would like continuing prayer support. Pray with them over the phone.
3. **Equip**—Complete the Bible study.
4. **Pray**—Pray that each couple would have the freedom and focus to prayerfully consider each other and how the challenges of the blended marriage have affected them. Pray that God will continue to give them the grace and strength they need to thrive in their blended marriage.

Session Three | Living with New Relationships

Before the Meeting

1. Gather materials for making name tags in addition to extra pens, paper, 3x5-inch index cards and Bibles.
2. Make photocopies of the Prayer Request Form, or provide index cards for recording requests.
3. Read through your own answers from the session and mark the ones that you especially want to have the group discuss. Also highlight any key verses you feel are appropriate to share.
4. Prepare slips of paper with references for the verses that you will want someone to read aloud during the session. Distribute these slips as group members arrive, but be sensitive to those who are uncomfortable reading aloud or who might not be familiar with the Bible.
5. Have a kitchen blender sitting on a table as a focal point. Also bring a recipe for a fruit smoothie and a recipe for another type of food and the ingredients for each recipe. These will be used during the ice breaker.

Ice Breakers

1. Hand a Prayer Request Form (or index card) to each member as he or she enters the room. Encourage members to at least fill in their name and phone number, even if they don't have any requests. Remind members that everyone needs someone to pray for them, even if there is no specific need.
2. Use the blender as a visual aid to remind each couple that when they came together in a blended relationship, others were thrown into the container with them: all other relatives, pets, children, memories, traditions, etc.

    Explain that you are going to make a fruit smoothie. Then start adding the ingredients, but part way through the recipe switch to the other recipe and start adding some of those ingredients (this would be especially effective if the second recipe has onions, garlic or other smelly ingredients). Someone will probably protest. If not, go ahead and blend the ingredients from both recipes, and then ask if anyone would like to taste the concoction. Explain that when we are blending our families we need to follow the recipe—God's Word—to make the blend palatable.

3. Invite couples to share what the visual of the blender and the mixed-up recipes invokes in them.

Discussion

1. **Tilling the Ground**—Discuss questions 1 and 2. Question 3 can be discussed by the couples during the Harvesting the Fruit time.
2. **Planting the Seed**—Lead the whole group through the Bible study discussion.
3. **Watering the Hope**—Discuss this section as a group, inviting volunteers to share their thoughts on the questions.
4. **Harvesting the Fruit**—Have individual couples share their answers in private. In closing, read the 10 rules for confident stepparenting and invite members to select the most helpful one, based on their own experience. If there is time, invite them to suggest additional rules.
5. **Close in Prayer**—Have each couple pair up with another couple and pray together. Invite them to swap prayer requests. Invite them to pray for the other couple in the coming week, contacting them via phone, e-mail or note.

After the Meeting

1. **Evaluate**—Spend time evaluating the meeting, noting what worked and what didn't work.
2. **Encourage**—Contact each couple during the week and see how they are doing. Ask if they have contacted their prayer partners.
3. **Equip**—Complete the Bible study.
4. **Pray**—Pray that each couple would have the conviction to surrender their new personal and family relationships to the Lord for His help and healing. Ask God to give each couple a desire to honor Him in all their relationships.

Session Four | Living with New Hope

Before the Meeting

1. Gather materials for making name tags in addition to extra pens, paper, 3x5-inch index cards and Bibles.
2. Make photocopies of the Prayer Request Form, or provide index cards for recording requests.
3. Make photocopies of the Study Review Form (see *The Focus on the Family Marriage Ministry Guide* "Reproducible Forms" section).
4. Read through your own answers from the session and mark the ones that you especially want to have the group discuss. Also highlight any key verses you feel are appropriate to share.
5. Prepare slips of paper with references for the verses that you will want someone to read aloud during the session. Distribute these slips as group members arrive, but be sensitive to those who are uncomfortable reading aloud or who might not be familiar with the Bible.
6. For the ice breaker, gather the makings of fresh lemonade: lemons, sugar, water and ice. Also gather the equipment: a large clear pitcher, a knife, a juicer (optional), a measuring cup and a long-handled spoon. If you aren't used to making fresh lemonade, practice making lemonade before the meeting. Set the materials up on a table at the front of the room. **Option**—Have lemonade prepared in advance so that each group member can have a glass of the real thing.

Ice Breakers

1. Give each member two Prayer Request Forms/index cards this week. One for prayer requests and the other for a praise report. Encourage them to write one thing God has done in them, as a couple or as a family, over the course of this study. Hand out Bible references on slips of paper for reading aloud later.
2. Begin the demonstration with an empty pitcher. Explain that at times we might think that life has handed us lemons in the form of trials or difficult relationships. Cut some lemons in half and squeeze the juice

into the pitcher. Continue by explaining that we can try to dilute the problems (add some water) or treating others coldly (add some ice), but our lives will continue to be sour. When we add God's love to the mix (add sugar) and blend it altogether (stir), we get sweet, refreshing lemonade. At times new troubles will occur (cut more lemons and add the juice to the mix), and we have a choice: become bitter like this sour lemonade or allow God's love to overcome bitterness (add more sugar and stir). When life hands us lemons, we can choose whether to drink sour lemon juice or add the sweetness of God's love to make the blend more palatable.

3. Invite couples to share the hope that comes with acknowledging their need for God's love in blending their families.

Discussion

1. **Tilling the Ground**—Discuss questions 1 through 3.
2. **Planting the Seed**—Divide into groups by gender and have each group discuss the questions.
3. **Watering the Hope**—Discuss questions 23 through 26 with the whole group. Invite volunteers to share their thoughts on question 27.
4. **Harvesting the Fruit**—Allow time for each couple to share their answers privately. Suggest that they focus on the hope they can share in making new choices through God's strength.
5. **Close in Prayer**—Since this is the final meeting, have each couple share something from the study that has impacted them. Have each couple read their prayer requests and their praises. After each couple has shared, pray together as a group, in a circle, allowing time for praise and intercession.

After the Meeting

1. **Evaluate**—Distribute the Study Review Forms for members to take home with them. Emphasize the importance of feedback, and ask members to take the time this week to write their review of the group meetings and then to return them to you.
2. **Encourage**—Call each couple during the next week and invite them to

join you for the next study in the *Focus on the Family Marriage Series*.

3. **Equip**—Begin preparing and brainstorming new activities for the next Bible study.

4. **Pray**—Praise the Lord for the work He has done in the lives of the couples in the study. Continue to pray for these couples as they apply the lessons learned in the last few weeks.

Welcome to the Family!

As you participate in the *Focus on the Family Marriage Series*, it is our prayerful hope that God will deepen your understanding of His plan for marriage and that He will strengthen your marriage relationship.

This series is just one of the many helpful, insightful, and encouraging resources produced by Focus on the Family. In fact, that's what Focus on the Family is all about—providing inspiration, information, and biblically based advice to people in all stages of life.

It began in 1977 with the vision of one man, Dr. James Dobson, a licensed psychologist and author of 18 best-selling books on marriage, parenting, and family. Alarmed by the societal, political, and economic pressures that were threatening the existence of the American family, Dr. Dobson founded Focus on the Family with one employee and a once-a-week radio broadcast aired on only 36 stations.

Now an international organization, the ministry is dedicated to preserving Judeo-Christian values and strengthening and encouraging families through the life-changing message of Jesus Christ. Focus ministries reach families worldwide through 10 separate radio broadcasts, two television news features, 13 publications, 18 Web sites, and a steady series of books and award-winning films and videos for people of all ages and interests.

We'd love to hear from you!

For more information about the ministry, or if we can be of help to your family, simply write to Focus on the Family, Colorado Springs, CO 80995 or call 1-800-A-FAMILY (1-800-232-6459). Friends in Canada may write Focus on the Family, P.O. Box 9800, Stn. Terminal, Vancouver, B.C. V6B 4G3 or call 1-800-661-9800. Visit our Web site—www.family.org—to learn more about Focus on the Family or to find out if there is an associate office in your country.